Featherstone

Martin Pace

I LOVE
FOREST
SCHOOL

Transforming early years practice
through woodland experiences

Featherstone Education
An imprint of Bloomsbury Publishing Plc

50 Bedford Square
London
WC1B 3DP
UK

1385 Broadway
New York
NY 10018
USA

www.bloomsbury.com

Bloomsbury is a registered trade mark of Bloomsbury Publishing Plc

First published 2014

British Library Cataloguing-in-Publication Data
A catalogue record for this book is available from the British Library.

ISBN:
PB 978-1-4729-0607-6
ePDF 978-1-4729-0737-0

Library of Congress Cataloging-in-Publication Data
A catalog record for this book is available from the Library of Congress.

1 3 5 7 9 10 8 6 4 2

Printed and bound in India by Replika Press Pvt. Ltd

This book is produced using paper that is made from wood grown in managed, sustainable
forests. It is natural, renewable and recyclable. The logging and manufacturing processes
conform to the environmental regulations of the country of origin.

To view more of our titles please visit www.bloomsbury.com

Contents

"I love Forest School."

*"What do you love about
Forest School?"*

"Everything!"

Rohana (aged 3½ years)

Preface

I am not a fanatic about the outdoors. I have friends who are. Their entrance halls are permanently bedecked with kagools, bobble hats and muddy boots, and they take every opportunity to get into the elements. I envy them, and try to spend more time outdoors. Any day I don't get outside always feels like a day wasted, and whenever I am in nature, especially in woodland, it always feels like home.

I grew up living on the edge of the Peak District and holidaying in the Lake District – as a child I would dam streams, explore forests and make fires (I'm the one in the cloud of smoke). Many precious moments in my childhood were stored from being in nature.

Although I am not obsessive about the outdoors I am passionate about ensuring that children (including my own) get the opportunity to experience nature. And I am concerned that they don't. Hence writing this book.

> *"For the first time in nearly four million years of history, we are effectively trapping children indoors."*
>
> Tim Gill, 'Bred in Captivity'

I would like to thank my grandmother for my love of working with children – she gave me space to learn for myself and helped me just when I needed it. She had endless patience and taught me that the simplest things – tidying the shed, watching butterflies, picking rhubarb, shopping for groceries, drawing maps – could be the most engaging. When I discovered Mihaly Csikszentmihalyi's concept of 'flow', I understood why time spent with her was my happiest. It is to her that I dedicate this book.

MP, January 2014

Acknowledgements

A huge thank you to the children who feature in this book for their shared experiences. The staff team and parents, past and present, at Reflections Nursery and Forest School, Worthing, especially: Lyndsey Ridgwell, Shelley Barton, Harrie Jones, Yvonne Barr, Teresa Grimaldi, Angela Chick, Jessica Wild, Kathryn Jordan, Sarah Wood; and Linda Thornton and Pat Brunton. Thanks to teachers and families of the infant-toddler centres and pre-schools of Reggio Emilia, and especially to Stefano Sturloni of Salvador Allende pre-school, for inspirational indoor and outdoor work. I would also like to thank: Archimedes Training and Sarah Blackwell; the Secret Garden Outdoor Nursery and Cathy Bache; Chelsea Open Air Nursery and Kathryn Solly; and the forest and nature nurseries of Denmark. Peter and Ruth Parker for canoeing, caving, camping and climbing. And of course, Louise, Jess, Leila and Charlie.

Ice window in a stick wall

Introduction

Children in the outdoors: a rationale

...And yet one sees dim houses behind whose windows and doors thirty to forty little ones are penned in Day Nurseries.

Margaret McMillan, 1930

Our role as adults working with children is to give them the best possible care and education we can. Of course, the issue is: what is 'best'? In my lifelong journey towards a personal rationale for pedagogy, the words of Margaret McMillan, pioneer in early childhood, resonate strongly. I have visited the world-renowned pre-schools and infant-toddler centres of Reggio Emilia on eight study tours since 2003, where I have seen and been inspired by what are surely the finest nurseries on the planet, and the influence of the Reggio Approach on my understanding and practice has been immense. Yet there is no doubt that the outdoors offers something that no classroom can. As Marjorie Ouvry, author of *Exercising Muscles and Minds* says, some opportunities for learning only happen outside.

Children playing outdoors is not a new concept. As regular conference attendees will know, it is almost impossible to attend a seminar about outdoor learning without being asked to close your eyes and recall your first memory when playing as a child. These memories are invariably of experiences located in the outdoors, perhaps on a beach or in the garden at home. What is new is the resurgence in passion amongst educators for ensuring that the next generation get their share of outdoor play, and a rebalancing of attitudes towards riskier play. And it is much needed. Research shows that children are not getting out as much as their parents did:

> "Children spend less time playing in natural places, such as woodlands, countryside and heaths, than they did in previous generations. Less than 10% play in such places compared to 40% of adults when they were young."
>
> **Report to Natural England on Childhood and Nature: A survey on changing relationships with nature across generations, 2009**

Richard Louv, author of *Last Child in the Woods,* coined the phrase "nature-deficit disorder" to describe the negative consequences to individual health and to society as a whole as children have less and less physical contact with the natural world, and in particular just 'being' in nature. Risks to individual children are potentially: attention disorders, obesity, dampening of creativity, and depression. Tim Gill, author of *No Fear*, highlights the same concerns and refers to children being "bred in captivity".

Sunbeams and smoke in Reflections' forest

Children are playing outdoors less, and we ignore the potential dangers of this at our peril. Jan White, author of *Playing and Learning Outdoors*, points to the many benefits, making the case for the outdoors being critical to children's learning, by offering: exuberance, fresh air, feeling the elements and weather, contact with natural and living things to support their curiosity, freedom, real-world experiences, endless opportunities for discovery, whole-body involvement, emotional and mental well-being, social interactions, and challenge.

There are innumerable benefits of taking children into woodland but, as prosaic as it may sound, just the fact that there is nothing to break or damage, nothing to keep in order or to keep clean, will often immediately relax children and adults alike and give a sense of freedom to any endeavour.

So is this book another rallying cry to get children into the outdoors? Absolutely it is. Because we have seen how it works.

Before you start

There is now a plethora of excellent outdoor learning and Forest School books covering many aspects of practice, which I will try to avoid re-hashing in this book. I will however, occasionally refer to some and point you in the direction of others.

I make little apology for the fact that much of my source material has been drawn from experiences at the nursery I work in – Reflections Nursery and Forest School in Worthing, West Sussex, UK. I do refer to other settings briefly and these include: The Secret Garden Outdoor Nursery, Chelsea Open Air Nursery, and some of the forest and nature nurseries in Denmark. I readily acknowledge the limitations of focusing on the experiences at Reflections but I have elected to offer a deeper look at the work we have been involved in rather than a broader perspective. In short, I have chosen depth over breadth.

This book is not intended as a practical guide. Its purpose is simply to relate experiences of educators and children in the outdoors and hopefully inspire or support your thinking regarding the importance of choices. Education involves making choices. Whatever choices we make as educators will be based on our philosophical, ethical, political and pedagogical values. So this is absolutely not a 'how to...' book, but rather an opportunity to share my values as an educator, to show examples of why we choose to run a Forest School programme at Reflections, and the significant influence it has had on our understanding and the further choices we make for children.

Den building in Reflections' forest

What is this book about?

'Forest School' is a name with connotations, but I have chosen to stick with it for this book on the basis that, taking into account the meaning it carries, it is a fair description of what we do at Reflections whilst still allowing for flexibility of approach. Chapter 1 looks at what defines Forest School and what experiences children engage with. There is a very short history of Forest School, and the significance of the Danish approach to outdoor learning is discussed and how it has influenced practice in the UK since the early 1990s. There is now much research making the case for Forest School and Helen Tovey, author of *Playing Outdoors*, covers this well. This chapter includes but a brief reference to the research.

At Reflections Nursery we draw inspiration from the pre-schools of Reggio Emilia in Northern Italy. Whilst the Reggio Approach significantly influences our values and practice including our approach to Forest School, Reggio is not renowned for its outdoor learning. In this we have been influenced by our Forest School training and other outdoor experiences, including the Forest Schools of Denmark, which are referred to in Chapter 2. There is a short description of a visit to the Secret Garden Outdoor Nursery in Fife, along with visits to three forest nurseries in Denmark by way of examples of wonderful environments and some inspired practice. Chapter 2 also touches on how Forest School does not always need to involve a 'forest'.

Reflections Nursery and Forest School

In Chapter 5, the 'ripple effects' of Forest School experiences are discussed, including how they have significantly influenced our nursery environment and our approach to risk in nursery. There is mention of our Edible Garden, which has been influenced by our more intimate relationship with nature. Forest School has had a transformational effect on our practice and Chapter 5 includes an excerpt from a project showing the experiences of two children, Teddy and Leila, which elucidates this. The project was a conversation between the indoor environment in nursery, the nursery garden and the woodland, and went on to further influence the nursery garden through a woodland-inspired design by the children.

Hugo, tree climbing

Chapter 3 covers how Reflections Nursery has drawn from the Reggio Approach. Included is an example of children's project work in the nursery garden, which pointed the way towards starting our Forest School programme. And to show how our forest programme progressed over time there is a section about the practicalities of launching Forest School at Reflections. Our pedagogical approach is elaborated upon and includes numerous examples of how our forest work follows this approach.

Risky play is critical to children's development. If we accept the image of the child as rich in potential, active, strong, powerful, competent and capable of directing their own learning and play, then what naturally flows from this for us as educators is, what challenges do we need to ensure they encounter? The significance of risk in play is explored in Chapter 4 along with our approach at Reflections and how that has developed through experience, including our recent of adoption of what Tim Gill refers to as a 'dynamic risk assessment approach'.

Thomas playing 'peepo'

Please note that, throughout, the book only refers to the experiences of children in the early years: that is, up to 5 years old. Many infant, primary and secondary schools offer Forest School or similar outdoor experiences, but this book will not cover their work. Children's ages, where shown, are referred to using (years:months), e.g. (2:8) would refer to a child aged 2 years and 8 months. Unless stated otherwise, all children featured in this book are either 3 or 4 years old.

What is Forest School?

> *Must we always teach our children with books? Let them look at the mountains and the stars up above. Let them look at the beauty of the waters and the trees and flowers on earth. They will then begin to think, and to think is the beginning of a real education.*

David Polis, Environmentalist and Outdoor Educator[viii]

Defining 'Forest School'

'Forest School' is a loaded term – it carries specific meaning, or expectations. The Forest Education Initiative , Sara Knight and others have offered definitions for those wishing to use the term Forest School with impunity. The main principles are as follows:

1. The setting is not the usual one – it is an outdoor area defined as the Forest School space. Woodland, within travelling distance of the nursery, is ideal.

2. Forest School is about learning in the outdoors, rather than learning about the outdoors (although of course it can encompass both).

3. Forest School experiences are about play and are child-led as far as possible.

4. It is a sustained or regular experience, generally once a week for at least 12 weeks.

5. The Forest School environment is made safe enough for children to take their own risks.

6. Children attend in all weathers, wearing appropriate clothing.

7. Staff are trained in Forest School practice by any of the accredited training organisations.

Sara Knight adds two further criteria, which give strong guidance to good practice:

8. The blocks (programme) and sessions have clear beginnings and ends – to give a sense that something special is about to happen or has happened.

9. Trust is central – adults and children trust each other to follow the rules.

Of course there are settings in the UK that might describe themselves as Forest Schools, not all of which meet the criteria above, and I make no criticism of that. And the terminology 'Forest School' encompasses a very wide range of experiences, even within the definitions above. I would choose to highlight one of the key elements, which might not be explicit in the above definitions, but which Sara Knight, author of *Forest Schools and Outdoor Learning in the Early Years*, recognises – that Forest School is special. Whatever the experience, there is a sense that it is a special time; even if it happens every day. The adult educators' excitement and passion should support this too. My view is that there is no room for the blasé when working with children – their awe and wonder should never be devalued.

A short history of Forest School

Much has been written about the historical connections by Knight (2009), Doyle and Milchem (2012), Williams-Siegfredsen (2012), and Constable (2012) but Forest Schools can trace their inspiration and ancestry from various roots, with influences from Pestalozzi, Froebel, Thompson Seton, Baden-Powell, McMillan, Isaacs and Hahn. As early as 1854, shortly after the first Froebel school opened in Denmark, the headmaster Søren Sørensen advocated the concept of children learning in the outdoors:

> *"Children at the ages or 4 and 5 years should not be imprisoned in a dirty airless schoolroom, at such a young age they should have play and movement, especially in the fresh air".*

In Wisconsin in 1927, land was set aside in three areas for use as schools in the forest, operated by Wakelin McNeel, a youth leader. And in 1928 Natalie Davies, an American living in London, opened Chelsea Open Air Nursery School for her own children. The nursery offered a healthy and invigorating lifestyle and children quickly became used to playing outdoors in all weathers, whilst indoors the rooms were never heated to more than 13.3°C, the ideal temperature for active children. Over the years the school has been significantly influenced by Susan Isaacs and, until recently, in the capable hands of Kathryn Solly.

I mention Chelsea Open Air School (which does not call itself a Forest School) as an example of how a setting without access to a woodland and with a relatively small outdoor area can still provide a deeply engaging environment full of challenge for children. It emphasises the point that what we call Forest School is more of a philosophical, value-based approach giving scope for children's freedom, choice and risk taking, rather than a woodland environment.

Chelsea Open Air Nursery School and Children's Centre

What we know today as Forest School originated in Scandinavia in the 1950s. Since the late 1970s Danish pre-school children have had access to experiences which have much in common with UK early years Forest Schools. Influences on UK Forest Schools have been drawn principally from Denmark and it was on a study tour in 1993 that a group of educators from Bridgwater College in Somerset were inspired to incorporate many of the experiences they had seen in Danish settings into their own Early Years Children's Centre. Within a year of accessing what was little more than a playing field, the educators saw benefits in children's confidence, independence and self-esteem. In 1996 Bridgwater educators sourced areas of woodland and expanded their sessions. By 2000, Bridgwater College began to share their concept and provide accredited training and support, which has led to the Forest School movement in the UK today.

Forest Schools have become an important facet of education in early years and primary settings, and of course not all have direct access to woodland. As Karen Constable, author of *The Outdoor Classroom ages 3-7*, puts it: "Forest School has become an ethos rather than a place."

Garden shelter at Globussen nursery

Lessons from Denmark

It is worth considering what those educators from Bridgewater experienced in Denmark that so inspired them. Using the outdoors for health, play and education is part of a way of living for the Danish – it is referred to as 'friluftsliv', or 'fresh air life'. Over many years this concept has developed as a pedagogical approach.

There are now many types of forest or nature nurseries in Denmark, many of which tend to be nearby or adjacent to woodland, or else they have developed their own natural environment around the nursery, influenced by the forest.

The outdoor areas of these nurseries are rich with open-ended materials such as crates, tyres and logs. They have a fire pit, with cooking on the open fire perhaps once week. There are wooden shelters, large open sandpits and areas for digging. Children frequently have access to tools, which they are trained to use.

Even indoors, children have continuous opportunity to be physical and the connection with the outdoors is palpable.

What the Bridgwater educators witnessed were confident pre-school children who had an understanding and appreciation of nature. They accessed the resources with confidence, having been taught the skills where required and enjoyed freedom to make their own choices in their play.

Covered sand area, Globussen nursery

Fire pit at Lille Dalby

Using tools at Globussen

The much-used indoor climbing wall at Lille Dalby

Research – making the case for Forest School

There is much research to support the case for Forest School, which can easily be found on a quick internet search. There have been a number of studies conducted in England, Wales and Scotland, often by groups such as Forestry Research, a social and economic research group which found that children developed their confidence, social skills, language and communication skills, motivation, concentration, physical skills, and knowledge and understanding. The results of their study are outlined below, and most other studies support and echo these findings:

Confidence: *Characterised by self-confidence and self-belief that came from the children having the freedom, time and space, to learn, grown and demonstrate independence.*

Social Skills: *Children demonstrated an increased awareness of the consequences of their actions on other people, peers and adults, and acquired a better ability to work co-operatively with others.*

Language and Communication: *Children developed more sophisticated use of written and spoken language, prompted by their visual and sensory experiences at Forest School.*

Motivation and Concentration: *Characterised by a keenness to participate in exploratory learning and play activities as well as the ability to focus on specific tasks for extended periods of time.*

Physical Skills: *Children developed physical stamina and gross motor skills through free and easy movement round the Forest School site. They developed fine motor skills by making objects and structures.*

Knowledge and Understanding: *Increased respect for the environment was developed as well as an interest in their natural surroundings. Observational improvements were noted as the children started to identify flora and fauna.*

The same study found benefits for the educators in developing new perspectives and understanding of the children and the 'ripple effects' as children brought their experiences back to nursery and home, often influencing parent's views. (These factors are further explored in Chapter 5.)

A much-cited, Swedish 13-month study found that children attending Forest School kindergartens were far 'happier' than children in town kindergartens. The study concluded that children who attended forest pre-schools were more balanced and socially capable, had fewer sick days, were more able to concentrate and had better co-ordination than the town nursery children:

"When it comes to concentration capacity, the children within I Ur och Skur pre-schools are more than twice as focused as children within a normal pre-school. Their motor skills are better, they are less frustrated, restless and sick."

Patrick Grahn, University of Sweden

Down the mountain in Reflections' forest

Approaches to Forest School

" *'Outdoors' is different to 'indoors' and this is exactly why it matters to children.*

Jan White[xvi] "

All areas of the Early Years Foundation Stage (or Phase, in Wales) can be covered by Forest School experiences – but settings may each have a different focus depending on the environment, the resources, the skills, experiences and approach of the educators, and the interests of the children. Experiences will include any or all of the following: physical activities; imaginative play; theorising and problem-solving; flora, fauna and foraging; tools and skills; and creative expression.

What Forest Schools tend to have in common is that experiences are often child-led and children's independence, confidence and self-esteem grow:

> *"Forest School is an inspirational process that offers children regular opportunities to achieve and develop confidence and self-esteem through hands-on learning experiences in a local woodland environment."*
>
> **Forest Education Initiative**

This chapter will take a short look at some examples of children's experiences outdoors in three Danish forest nurseries: Høndruphus, Laerkereden and Globussen; and the Secret Garden Outdoor Nursery in Fife, by way of examples of different approaches.

Exploring flora at Høndruphus

Vine headresses at Høndruphus

Høndruphus Naturbørnehave (Nature Nursery)

In late September 2010 I joined a Sightlines Initiative study tour of six forest schools in Denmark. The first school we visited was extraordinary. Situated in an 18th century farmhouse (which is so remote that the road turns into a farm track before you arrive), Høndruphus Naturbørnehave is just outside a tiny hamlet called Lindum, near Tjele in the north of Denmark. It is run by a passionate pedagogue, Bitten Pedersen, and the setting is immediately adjacent to Lindum woods so children have direct access to acres of woodland and rolling hills.

During our stay here we saw children who were trusted to manage their own risk, enjoying the opportunity to develop their physical skills.

The track up to Høndruphus

Høndruphus from the woods

Rope bridge in the woods

Swinging in the woods

Children clearly valued the tranquility and beauty of the natural surroundings and used all their senses to investigate nature. After a delightful walk in the woodland observing spectacular fungi, one child found an animal skull. This was immediately recognised as a treasure and brought back to Bitten for dicussion and indentification.

Investigating flowers

Fly agarics in the woods

Once inside, the setting was full of examples of flora and fauna, and the children were able to compare the skull with those of animals which frequent the woodland. Bitten shared her passion for flora and fauna and referred to the joy of "looking into the eyes of a ladybird."

In the afternoon we were treated to a presentation (in English) by two confident older children who had attended Høndruphus a few years previously. It was clear from the presentation that they valued how much time they had been given to scaffold their own learning.

We know that giving children time is important in the early years, and many of us on the study tour commented on this. One visitor described the setting as "slow-pedagogy", a bit like slow food: better by far than fast food and much more considered. There was a sense that mind, body and soul were being nurtured here.

Finding a skull

Lærkereden Naturbørnehave (Nature Nursery)

The study tour included a visit to a setting in woodland near the coast - Lærkereden Naturbørnehave is the forest nursery part of a larger integrated setting on the tiny island of Thurø, near Svendborg.

As we arrived there was a lit fire with an outdoor lunch being prepared. There was evidence that during the morning the children had been foraging for fungi.

Fungi from the woodland

Fire pit and lunch

Open tool box for all

A four-year old, whittling

Hilvie learning skills

I spent some time observing three-year-old Hilvie, who was being shown how to use a knife. Her older friends were whittling away nearby and she was keen to join them. The educator explained that the toolbox is always available and children access whatever tools they like, provided they have been shown how to use them – a privelege respected by the children and trusted by the adults.

Respect and trust is a strong theme in Forest Schools, and I saw this encouraged and fostered by caring, nurturing adults in all the Danish settings, espeically here at Lærkereden.

Ryttergården og Globussen skovgruppe (forest group)

We visited a skovgruppe, who travel to the forest whilst still providing what most UK settings would call a woodland within its own grounds.

Giant nesting box and bird feeder

Trail through the fruit trees

Play netting in the school's wooded area

Swing in the school garden

School chickens

Ryttergården og Globussen is a setting in Svendborg that provides a rich outdoor learning environment. The centre comprises a school and nursery, and a modifed bus takes the children on a short drive to woodland by the coast. Children play games and draw en route on tables provided, and unpack tools on arrival. We observed a group of 5 year olds.

Carrying tools on arrival at the forest

Foraging up a tree

Once the children had arrived at the woodland, a fire was lit and they immediately engaged in imaginative play, climbing, foraging and working with tools. All the children seemed very adapted to the environment – I was taught how to forage for rosehips and apples by a 5 year old.

Other children worked on shaping sticks by the fire. There were clear rules about the beach area, which children respected and adults trusted them to do so.

The beach adjacent to the forest

Whittling together at Globussen

There were so many notable features about these three Danish settings and the quality of the educators and the environments that it seems an injustice to pick out a few. The whole experience was rich with calm, nurturing adults working in a mutally-trusting and respecful way with the children. There was lots of space, a wide range of natural, open-ended resources and children had the freedom to take risks and exercise their natural curiosity. What was also notable was that children had a deep sense of respect for nature and the environment.

The Secret Garden Outdoor Nursery, Fife

I was fortunate enough to spend a day with Cathy Bache at the Secret Garden in Fife. The nursery has operated since September 2008, receiving the Nancy Ovens Award for 'Outstanding Contribution to Play' and from Play Scotland, 'Best Practice in Action'.

Based in a 25-acre woodland, the nursery offers explorative outdoor play, 4½ days a week, for 49 weeks of the year from 8.30am - 5.00pm. The setting has no premises as such and I was curious to see how this worked. On very inclement days there is a small village hall that they can use; otherwise the whole experience is in the open air.

There were two educators on the day I attended, Cathy and Roz. Children began to arrive with their parents in a local park at 8.30am. When the group of 10 were assembled, complete with backpacks to carry their lunches, we made our way up the hill towards the woodland.

Up the hill to the forest

The Secret Garden has a Visitor Protocol , which says much about their approach. They ask you to be aware of "the power that the adult agenda may have in blocking the aspiration to free play", and advise visitors to stand well back from the play and act like David Attenborough 'animal watching'.

This was very much insisted upon by Cathy, and I stood back when observing children climbing and engaging in imaginative play. There were instances of children clambering over slippery rocks at some height, but they had clearly done this before. Other children were aware of the risks and offered safety advice that was sometimes heeded and often rebutted.

The children gathered for lunch, and there was much lively discussion about the morning session together with a gentle ritual in which they showed respect for the forest.

The group meets for lunch

Group discussion

The afternoon included some skills work with ropes and lots of play on the rope swing, whilst others further engaged in imaginative play. It was a chilly day and one or two children felt the cold. A small tent and blankets offered respite.

Before the end of the day in the forest, Roz had prepared a slideshow of the children's experiences, which she shared with all the children, crowded round the laptop.

The day in the forest ended with more gentle ritual then a walk back to the park. As we arrived it was already dark and one or two parents were waiting. The slideshow was made available for parents to watch at collection time, with lots of feedback from Roz and Cathy.

Throughout the day I noted how the children had a deep awareness of their own ability to handle risk, especially with regard to their physical activities. What is implicit in this is that regular attendance at the setting gives children the confidence and independence to cope with complex physical tasks.

Both Cathy and Roz showed a passion for their work, which translated into some wonderful experiences for the group, and their gentle respectfulness for nature and the woodland gave a magical tone to the whole day. What was also notable was a deep level of trust shown by the parents to the educators – it was as if everyone understood that this was a special experience.

Roz sharing photos of the day

Skills on the swing

Back down the hill

No access to woodland?

Katherine Milchem of Eastwood Nursery School in Roehampton makes the case eloquently for urban Forest Schools:

> *The outdoor environment offers children the freedom to explore, use their senses and be physically active and exuberant.*
>
> **Ofsted 2011**

> *"Many seem to think you need to be in the countryside to be able to do Forest School, when in actual fact, you don't. It's true that finding natural spaces in London can be more challenging, but it's vital that children growing up in the city also have access to learn through nature too. How else are children in the city meant to develop a personal morality towards nature, if they never have access to it in open spaces?"*

It is worth mentioning that any outdoor environment can offer opportunities for young children. Not everyone is fortunate enough to have access to a woodland environment but key elements can often be found in small areas of just a few trees or open land.

At Grangetown Nursery in the centre of Cardiff they have a small but meaningful space designated for their Forest School sessions, which provides wonderful experiences for the children and has significant influence on the educators' practice indoors.

At Reflections we have woodland within driving distance and choose to access it for our Forest School because it provides rich resources for young children: sticks, stones, ditches, hills, mud, water, ice, snow, and a sense of freedom. Nature herself contributes a continuously changing environment and new flora and fauna with each season.

'Forest' area, Grangetown Nursery, Cardiff

Some settings may have easier access to a beach area and are able to follow the forest approach there. There is specific training available through Archimedes and other training providers, tailoring the Forest School ethos for Beach School.

Arriving at the beach

Land art on the beach

Fia investigating treasure

Designing a whale

Whale at Reflections Beach School

What is Reflections' approach?

"

Our task is to help children climb their own mountains, as high as possible. No one can do more.

Loris Malaguzzi, Reggio Emilia[xxi]

"

Drawing inspiration from the Reggio Approach

Reflections Nursery draws inspiration from the world-renowned pre-schools and infant toddler centres of Reggio Emilia. I returned from my first study tour to Reggio in 2003 and wept. I wanted to be Italian, live in Reggio and teach in a Reggio school. A good friend and colleague, Linda Thornton, author of *Understanding the Reggio Approach*, gave me a quote from Aldo Fortunati which helped me deal with my grief: "Trust in the richness of your own context."

The mountain in snow at Reflections Forest School

I came to recognise that we have a rich pedagogical inheritance in the UK and that whilst we are not operating a nursery with the backing of the Municipality of Reggio Emilia and a 50-year experience of pedagogy driven by a visionary like Loris Malaguzzi, there is still much we can do.

Drawing inspiration from Reggio provides us with an opportunity to draw from a framework of reference points and a philosophical approach, still working within the context of our own pedagogical inheritance, culture, geography, financial constraints and national pedagogic guidelines.

For us at Reflections, it means we begin with the image of the child as: rich in potential, strong, powerful, competent, confident in building relationships, having values and respect for others, having a curiosity and open-mindedness to all that is possible and capable of independent, critical, divergent thinking.

If we hold this positive image of the child then what is the role of the adult? We see the educators' role as co-constructor of knowledge with the children. In Reggio the role of the teacher is "not to teach but to learn." What naturally ensues is that we listen to children. But listening in the deepest way possible, as Carlina Rinaldi explains:

> *"Listening means being open to what others have to say, listening to the hundred or more languages , with all our senses. Listening means being open to differences, and recognising the value of different points of view and the interpretations of others."*
>
> **Rinaldi 1999, Reggio Emilia**

Tree project – Reflections Nursery 2008/9

Listening to children's theories about the world and giving them the opportunity to investigate those theories tends to lead to long-term projects. Often initiated by the children, they form part of our pedagogical practice at Reflections and it was such a project, beginning with a tree in the nursery garden, which acted as a precursor to launching our Forest School programme.

In late 2008 there was a dead tree in Reflections' nursery garden. Knowing that whatever we did with the tree would significantly impact on the children's environment we decided to introduce all the children in the nursery to the tree. They were encouraged to explore the tree with all their senses.

Thomas observing the tree

Dead tree in Reflections' garden

Aoife and Amelie listening to the tree

Imogen, really listening to the tree

During these explorations, a group of 2, 3 and 4 year olds developed a deep sense of connection with the tree and began to have theories about what might have happened to it. The short study below relates the experiences of these children over a period of 6 months.

In a group discussion, children were concerned about the tree:

> "It might be died. It was here a long, long time…"
> **Angus (3:4)**

> "The tree is poorly."
> **Niamh (2:11)**

> "We need to help the tree, don't we?"
> **Amelie (3:6)**

> "Like a jumper! I wear a jumper when I'm cold and it's cold today so maybe the tree is cold!"
> **Angus (3:4)**

Prototype tree jumper

Making jumpers for the tree

Educators provided the children with resources and children set to work as a production line, creating 'jumpers' to make the tree warm and gifts to cheer it up. Jumpers and gifts were subsequently hung in the tree.

Dave, working on the tree

The artist who was working with the children (known in the Reggio approach as an Atelierista) arranged for two tree sculptors, Bill and Dave, to meet with the children to hear their views about the tree. It would be their role to make the tree safe and to carve it into something that respected the children's interests.

One child said he wanted to "play in the roots of the tree", and others took up this idea. Bill and Dave noted the children's deep connection with the tree and the gifts that had been made and decided to work the tree into a landscape for the children to interact with, including cubbyholes for gifts and ridges to wedge notes and drawings in.

Bill and Dave set to work with chainsaws, observed closely by a considerable audience of pre-school children who were working at tables around the tree.

Bill working with the chainsaw

These tables often consisted of girls who sat solemnly watching the tree be butchered, whilst taking pieces cut from the tree and decorating them as gifts which were later given back to the tree.

Rohana drawing on bark

Gifts for the tree

While visiting the garden, Ewa (2:11) asked to be lifted up and used her hand to hit a wind chime. This gave her friend Adam an idea:

> "Why don't we make one for birds that live in trees? They like music I think… and presents"
>
> Adam (3:1)

"Birds like shiny things"

The Atelierista provided the children with knives, forks, spoons, string and kitchenware, and they set about making a wind chime to attract the birds to the tree. During the process of manufacture the children saw an opportunity to make the tree feel better by including medicine in the string of the wind chime. The wind chime became a medicine dispenser:

> "We're making this for the tree because the tree is poorly. I need to wrap the medicine for the tree. I'll put it in the string so it can use the spoon for medicine."
>
> Niamh (2:11)

The project continued with further gifts including dances for and with the tree, silver conkers to attract the birds, and pretend leaves made from PVA-covered cabbage leaves – so the tree could be like the other trees.

> "Birds like shiny things"
>
> Adam (3:1)

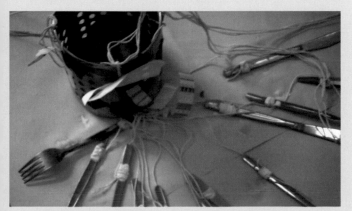

Designing the wind chime

Wind-chime medicine dispenser

Launching Forest School at Reflections Nursery

We frequently document long-term work like the tree project in the nursery, and reflecting on these projects often informs the next steps in our plans with the children. It was the children's deep sense of emotional connection with the dead tree in the nursery garden, alongside our conviction that the outdoors can offer another dimension to children's learning, which inspired us to look deeper into Forest School.

In 2009 we had discussions with parents and agreed that nine 3 and 4 year old children would attend a pilot programme of six three-hour sessions in local woodland used by Scouts and Guides, travelling by minibus each day.

I became our first Forest School leader following a Forest School Practitioner Level III course with Archimedes Training in Sheffield (also known as Forest Schools Education). The initial pilot sessions were hugely popular with the children and with parents, and following these introductory sessions we decided to launch a full Forest School programme for any children who wanted to go and whose parents agreed. We presented our plans to parents of 3 and 4 year olds in the nursery, explaining our approach, the practicalities of working in a woodland setting and dealing with any concerns – and there were a few, especially around the use of tools and fires.

Session 1, summer 2009

Megan in a tree

The first full programme was launched in October 2009 with 24 children in two groups of 12, two mornings a week, for 30 weeks, initially with four staff (which we later reduced to three – we found that with four staff the adults didn't stand back enough). After a short period in the Scouts and Guides' woodland we rented our own woodland, a 15-minute minibus ride from the nursery, from a local landowner for £50 per year.

Our site is a 6-acre wood which, although private, is adjacent to some public woodland. It is predominantly hazel with some chestnut, oak and birch and one very old yew (which we call the 'oldest tree' and tends to be our storytelling area). Hazel grows in clumps and falls over a lot so, apart from the potential dangers to the children, which we monitor, it is a wood very full of long straight branches, brilliant for children's den building.

We initially made a 'base' in the woodland with stick walls as windbreaks, log tables and even a log loo. However, we found that any camp which was near the public side of the wood quickly got vandalised:

> *"The table's gone."* **Rohana**
>
> *"The swing's gone. Aah!"* **Aoife**
>
> *"Look at our toilet!"* **Scarlett**
>
> *"An aeroplane done it...."* **Ryan**
>
> *"Someone burnt it down."* **Rohana**
>
> *"Someone had a fire and didn't put it out and the wind blew and burnt it down."* **Scarlett**
>
> *"It was a big naughty person who came in the night."* **Amelie**

We asked the children how they felt about it:

> *"I feel sad."* **Amelie**
>
> *"Sad and cross! AAAH!"* **Aoife** (shouting)

We have now found a clearing quite deep in the wood, which is rarely visited, and this is where we have our 'base' – a tarpaulin slung between trees and four logs as seating. Nearby, there are two ditches that the children use for imaginative play and traverse using branch bridges, and an excellent fallen tree for climbing. We have installed a rope swing and the children have made numerous dens that are erected and dismantled (usually to make another 'better' one) with regularity.

In the woodland we document children's experiences – one adult takes notes and another carries a camera or video recorder. From these notes and photos we select key themes for a daily diary. These provide us as educators with an excellent tool for reflecting on interests and dispositions in the woodland. By keeping track of learning journeys in the form of the diary, the Forest School educators can assess when to step in to support or to provoke a next step.

The diary is emailed to parents on the same day as their child's session so that they can discuss their child's woodland experiences, and always comprises four pages of photographs, narrative and quotations from the children.

Playing near base

Ditches near base

Tree climbing near base

We frequently get feedback from parents and children when they are reading the diary together at home:

"A message from the twins: 'Thank you for bringing us to Forest School, we loved putting the other stick across the hole for the bridge and looking for the treasure. We had a lovely time.' Thank you for fostering the engineer and the treasure hunter in our children! They had a great time and really enjoyed sharing their diary with us tonight."

Parent of twins at Reflections Forest School

A Forest School diary sample

Our Forest School programme has developed such that we now operate 5 mornings a week, taking 55 children in five groups, for three hours a day. The Forest School Leader supports every session and is accompanied by two further staff, selected from the Reflections team. Four members of staff have been Forest School trained, and all staff have qualifications in childcare and education.

The programme operates 44 weeks a year, taking only 2 weeks off at Christmas and 6 weeks in the summer. We choose to have a break during these periods as many children take holidays and a smaller learning group changes the dynamic. In addition, children who might be engaged with a long-term project could miss out on a critical stage of its development if they are away.

At Reflections what we offer children meets the definition of Forest School, but I would simply describe these experiences as children playing in woodland. I refer to playing, rather than 'working' or 'learning', but in relation to young children we see these terms as synonymous.

We found there were benefits to starting our Forest School programme in a small way. One group of nine children for just six weeks gave us the opportunity to develop skills and confidence in the team and deal with any concerns. Parents too, needed to learn to trust us with their children in the wider context outside the nursery environment. Our Forest School programme has developed over a period of several years, giving us the opportunity to scale up without losing our way. The growth in the number of children attending the sessions is representative of the trust and confidence the parents have in our approach.

It is worth noting that we take the same children in each group into the forest each week, by design. The principle motives for this are that we find children bond better in a consistent group – relationships forged in the woodland seem to be very strong. It also gives continuity to learning experiences and especially to project work. Perhaps most significantly, children quickly recognise each other's competencies and call on those, as required – an affirming experience for the individual. A small example of this can be seen in Lachlan and Kyra's interactions below:

The children were en route to camp when Lachlan pointed out a hawthorn tree to Kyra.

> *"Hawthorn. We can eat this!"*
>
> **Lachlan**

Kyra hadn't tasted hawthorn before and wanted to try the leaves, but couldn't reach. Lachlan kindly helped by bending the tree so Kyra could choose a leaf.

Hawthorn foraging

We have found that being in the forest is different. It can change mood in adults and children – there can be a sense of expectation, discovery and wonder, but it can also raise anxieties. When children first encounter woodland some will be keen to explore but others may be a little more hesitant. If they have not been in woodland before they may also have expectations that don't match the reality:

> *"We don't have any toys to play with!"*
>
> **Elliot**

In our experience, children who may be a little anxious in the early days will often find ways of dealing with this anxiety for themselves. For example, there had been talk of giants amongst the children and Angus, a boy with a very vivid imagination, had been concerned about this. It was quite dark in the forest but he decided that he was going to walk through the undergrowth like a "scary giant" and took big, confident, stomping steps. Following this there was much play about scary giants, which Angus happily engaged in.

The majority of nursery parents report that their children wake up and ask if it's a Forest School day, and are disappointed when it isn't. However, Forest School may not be every child's first choice. In five years of running over 500 Forest School sessions with 200 children, we have had four children request that they drop out of the programme. It is quite difficult to ascertain the exact reason each time but we believe that there may be a few factors affecting their choice:

- Firstly, children can get deeply involved in project work in nursery and perhaps would rather continue their investigations indoors and in the nursery garden.

- They may have other attachments to children and adults that are stronger than those of the Forest School group.

- They may simply be put off by the experience of going out in all weathers when it can be cosier inside.

- And the process of preparation, which includes the effort of getting dressed in warm and waterproof clothing on wet or cold days, may also be tiresome (although it is often filled with excited anticipation and lively discussion).

Whatever the reason, some children decide that Forest School is not for them and we always respect those decisions.

Reflections' approach

In Reggio Emilia there is an expression that "the environment is the third teacher" – the first teacher being the adult, and the second being the other children. This phrase gives significance to the environment (and resources) that children encounter on a daily basis. In my view there is no richer environment to offer a child than the forest where they can access a wide range of resources and need only their imagination and experience. And it is in recognition of nature as a teacher and as an environment, providing endless opportunity for enquiry, that we choose to offer outdoor experiences as frequently as possible at Reflections.

There are a number of theoretical influences underpinning the Forest School approach in general, and the pedagogical approach in Denmark, including: Pestalozzi, Froebel, Dewey, Montessori, Piaget, Vygotsky and Gardner. These theorists are also significantly influential in the history of the Reggio Approach. Before launching our Forest School programme we were concerned to ensure that our woodland work would fit with our values and pedagogy at Reflections. From the outset, we recognised that there need be no cause for concern.

Forest School training involves three elements – practical skills, knowledge of flora and fauna, and pedagogy – and it was clear that the Forest School pedagogical elements would not present any conflicting messages to children and educators, and could potentially add another dimension to our work.

The critical issue in our work with children is knowing when or when not to intervene. At Reflections, we try to intervene with children only when either overcoming obstacles or developing skills. From the schematic diagram below you will see that we tend to begin with a provocation, something designed to get children thinking or theorising.

So, in the case of the tree project we simply introduced the children to a dead tree as a provocation. We subsequently listened to their theories and provided them with the tools and resources to explore those theories. We documented the project on an ongoing basis and made choices about which paths to follow and how we might support children's learning. Reviewing the documentation later, we recognise that perhaps there was much more we could have done or different choices we could have made. That is the beauty of hindsight and where the learning lies for us as educators.

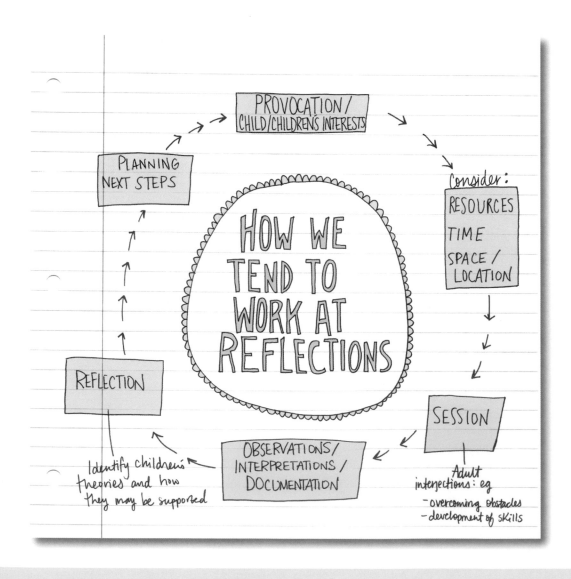

Provocations and interventions

Every day children find their own provocations in the forest. Their natural curiosity and innate ability to learn for themselves makes every 'found' object a significant part of their learning experience. Such as a tyre...

"Someone help me with this!" **Lachlan**

Lachlan subsequently refused help from the others and took great pride in carrying the tyre up the hill by himself.

Or chalk... which makes for wonderful mark-making...

"It can draw patterns. It's a drawing one."
Aidan, referring to his chalk

...and of course sticks make for great literacy opportunities:

"I've made an 'A'.... 'A' for Aidan!"
Aidan

In the woodland, we find that there is often even less need for us to intervene – so much of children's play is imaginative and we do not want to "cast an adult shadow over play that is free-flowing." (Tina Bruce).

Fire making (Reflections 2011)

By way of an example of intervening or not intervening with children, I have included an extract from some of the forest dairies following two children playing at making a fire. We have fires in the woodland whenever it is cold, and throughout the winter we will often cook on the fire for the children.

One week, Noa and Kiera began building an alternative base nearby our adult-built base in the woodland, after spotting a rotten tree stump that they considered ideal for a fire.

Pancakes on the fire

Forest Diary – Week 19

Noa (4:8) and Kiera (4:6) found an old tree stump and began excavating it. They decided it would make a good fireplace. Martin was building a fire in the base nearby.

> *"Can we have some sticks for our little fire?"*
> **Noa (to Martin)**

> *"We can have our lunch here can't we? Around our fire."*
> **Kiera**

Kiera identified a difference between the adult-built camp with its tarpaulin and their new, open-air camp:

> *"There is a problem though – we don't have a roof!"*
> **Kiera**

Some of the children helped collect sticks, and Noa borrowed the fire steel and tried to light their fire. Harry and Erin tried, too. Martin offered some help with the fire by providing some tumble-drier fluff. The children lit a fire together but it didn't last.

They began to create a 'fire square' around the fire and collected logs for seating.

> *"We need to make seats and then we can eat lunch here."*
> **Kiera**

All the children helped build the seating around the new fireplace. We ate our lunch around the new base, built by the children.

A week later, Noa and Kiera introduced the camp they had built to an adult, Robyn, who had not been present the previous week.

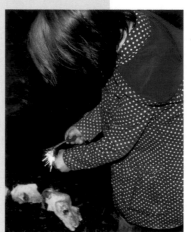

Noa using fire steel

Fire building

Noa and Kiera's fireplace

Forest Diary – Week 19

Noa and Kiera were keen to show Robyn their base, which they had built the week before:

> *"Robyn, we have a new camp to show you!"* **Noa**

They began to build a fire in their new base and asked Kyra (4:7) if she wanted to join them.

> *"We are going to get new wood for it."* **Noa**
>
> *"Kyra, that's too bendy; much too bendy."* **Kiera (referring to some live wood Kyra was offering for the fire).**

On week 20, the group visited a different part of the Forest; but by week 21 Noa and Kiera were back revisiting their fireplace and the base they had constructed, and were again investigating the tree stump their fire was based on.

By week 22, the stump had become a melting pot for making 'chocolate' and had spawned many imitations by other children who were building the basis of fires on tree stumps nearby.

By week 23, Noa and Kiera had made mud pies in their tree stump and had succeeded in lighting a fire (with adult supervision, but not help) on which we cooked lunch.

In the following weeks it rained and their investigations continued, focussing on building a roof to protect their new base from the elements.

Noa and Kiera roof–building

Noa and Kiera making mud pies

Knowing when (and when not) to intervene to support children's learning as they encounter obstacles is what they describe in Reggio Emilia as a '10-year apprenticeship' – and we don't always get it right. Forest School offers many self-directed learning opportunities and, provided sessions can be offered on a weekly basis and for long enough, children will independently scaffold their own learning.

Mammoth trap (Reflections 2010)

An example of an unintended provocation came when I fell in a ditch during one of the sessions.

Children often engage in problem solving in the forest, and even just manoeuvring large branches through the trees calls for lots of negotiation and teamwork.

We found an old oil drum, which from past experience the children will often roll into a ditch and then spend a session working out how to extricate it.

During a session on week 11 of the programme, there had been talk of mammoths en route to the forest and a group of children were on the lookout for one.

They were crossing one of the ditches using a homemade bridge when I stumbled and fell, much to the amusement of the children and adults.

A group of 3 and 4 year olds set about putting branches over the shallower ditch to trap any mammoths that might fall in.

> *"Mammoth trap! That looks really cool!"* **Angus**

Oliver had an idea to trip the mammoth up to make him fall into the ditch. Adam, Phoebe and Ben helped hammer stakes next to the trap.

Everyone was working hard on the mammoth trap when Ben had a suggestion:

> *"Can we put big logs in there?"* **Ben**
>
> *"It will hurt his knee."* **Angus**
>
> *"The Mammoth's going to be upset when he goes on those sticks."* **Ben**

As they were building the trap they decided to test it using the oil drum.

A few finishing touches, and the trap was laid.

We all hid and called to any mammoths to see if they would fall in. There was much discussion and some disagreement about what a mammoth was.

To the astonishment of the other children, who were all feeling a little nervous about catching a mammoth, Oliver went bravely to see if we had caught one. He called to us, peering over the edge of the trap:

> *"Nothing yet..."* **Oliver**

Martin falling in the ditch

Manoeuvring branches

Exploring the barrel

Stakes to trip a mammoth

Having not caught a mammoth, the children decided to use the trap to catch each other.

Laying the trap

The trap, laid

What is a mammoth?

Thomas getting trapped

Caught in the trap

Dead fox theories (Reflections 2010)

Natural provocations abound in the forest, but the children's imaginations were captured when we were making our way through the woods and found a dead fox.

The fox was a delightful find as an unplanned provocation, and there are many similarities between this and the dead rabbit experience that Susan Isaacs documented at Maltings House School over 70 years ago. As Isaacs experienced, there was much theorising and discussion:

> *"He's squashed. He looks kind of flat."* **Scarlett**
>
> *"He's not dead, he's dying."* **Thomas**
>
> *"His body's down here but the rest of him has gone to heaven."* **Amelie**

The children noticed lots of insects on the fox.

> *"Maybe they're going to make him better."* **Amelie**
>
> *"Maybe it was bad fox... Why is it smelly?"* **Scarlett**
>
> *"Maybe it's smelly coz the flies are on it."* **Amelia**
>
> *"Maybe it's the insects that are smelly?"* **Rohana**
>
> *"A nasty hunter came with his axe and chopped him."* **Lucas**

> *"Maybe he trod on some broken glass and his foot was sore and then he was dead."* **Amelia (probably a reference to our discussions about the danger of broken glass in the woods)**
>
> *"Maybe he ate food he wasn't meant to eat. Or maybe a Gruffalo ate it coz his favourite food is roasted fox!"* **Rohana**
>
> *"It's a skunk because they are really stinky."* **Angus**
>
> *"...No. It's a doggy and it just died."* **Adam**
>
> *"He died coz there's a stick in his tummy."* **Ben**

We asked the children how they knew the fox was dead.

> *"It's not moving."* **Katie**
>
> *"It's smelly and pooey."* **Adam**

Over the next few days, the children were keen to revisit the fox and noticed it disappearing quite quickly. At one point the fox was so ridden with maggots that its body was moving. This prompted more theorising about whether the fox was indeed dead. When there was very little of the fox left, the children were keen to understand where it had all gone:

> *"He's been eaten by lots of tiny, tiny bugs and they've gone off and now he's all over the forest."* **Amelie**

Back in the nursery, our next steps were to support the children's interest in decay with dead and dying flowers and rotting fruit and vegetables.

Investigating the dead fox

The fox becomes smelly

Mythologies in the woodland

There is often much storytelling in the woodland by adults and by children. More adult-directed experiences tend to involve us telling stories or hiding treasure and the children often continue these stories, creating their own mythologies.

The open-ended nature of the resources in the woodland gives rise to much creative expression, and in response to an adult story about fairies' dens being damaged or broken they will spend much time rebuilding (and later refining) fairy houses, and adding details such as patterned leaf trails to show the fairies the way.

> "Make a little path to their home so they know where they have been and where their home is.". Amelie
>
> "We could make a path out of my yellow leaves." Amelia

These mythologies are often about features in the woodland such as the 'dinosaur footprint', a moss-covered tree stump with outspread roots and the 'oldest tree' (where Santa had rescued his elves one night!). The children will use these reference points when navigating in the forest and will tell stories involving these features.

Serendipitous finds are especially useful provocations, so when we found a discarded sledgehammer in the forest we narrated a tale about Thor's hammer and the fairies hiding it from him so he doesn't inadvertently knock down their fairy dens.

This story has been revisited many times and usually includes a visit to the hammer and re-hiding it to make sure Thor really can't find it.

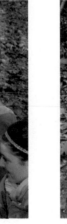

Amelia's triangle

Storytelling by the children

Dinosaur footprint

Fairy leaf trail

Thor's hammer

Mythologies in the woodland: trolls (Reflections 2013)

Many of the children's mythologies cross the boundaries of nursery to forest and back, and in 2013 'trolls' featured very large both indoors and outdoors. Children had been making bridges in the Atelier and the story of The Three Billy Goats Gruff featured in their play. Teresa, our Atelierista, planted a puppet troll outside by the Atelier window under the back stairs that the Forest School groups use to access the minibus.

The children passed up and down the stairs for quite some time before anyone noticed the troll, until one day:

> *"Look, there's a troll. I can see it!"* Yasmin

Once he had been spotted, there ensued a number of theories about where he had come from and lots of communication with the troll. A long tube was constructed from the corner of the Atelier through a pipe in the wall to talk to the troll and post letters to him.

The troll evoked some very ambivalent feelings which the children explored, working out whether he was friend or foe. One afternoon, after it had rained, the troll was oozing rainwater. Yasmin decided he must have had a "wee accident", and after this revelation the children began to warm to him.

In the nursery, the children drew and painted trolls and made trolls out of modelling materials:

> *"The dark troll! I'm making the dark troll!"* Teddy

The troll under the steps

Letters down the troll tube

Troll sculpture

Dark Troll

Troll letter

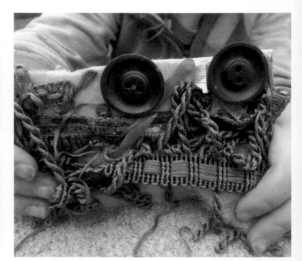

Button roll

Children began to see trolls in everything, including an Agate slice in the Atelier. In the woodland, children were seeing trolls in tree shapes.

> *"A troll's face!"* **Frankie**

Eventually, our resident troll at nursery made a trip into the forest with the children and was looked after during snack time.

> *"This is new to him, but not to us. It's old to us."* **Harriet**
>
> *"Troll doesn't have any food."* **Amelie**

Later, he was put to work under their bridge – where all good trolls reside.

> *"Who's that trip trapping over my bridge?"* **Phoenix**

Brick troll

Troll tree

Troll in agate slice

The troll has a snack in the forest

Troll under the children's bridge

Risks and benefits in the woodland

> *Risk-taking is an essential feature of play provision, and of all environments in which children legitimately spend time at play.*
>
> **Play England**[xxix]

Rusty car (Reflections 2013)

The photo below seems to cause a bit of a stir when presented at conferences. It divides educators on whether climbing in a rusty car is a suitable experience for pre-school children, or whether it is deemed as too 'risky'.

Firstly, let us differentiate between 'hazard' and 'risk'. A hazard is a physical situation which could be potentially harmful. Risk is the probability that a hazard will cause harm. The rusty car could potentially present a number of hazards: is it stable? Are there sharp edges, wire or glass? Is there any evidence of toxic chemicals? But what are the actual risks?

To set the image and the argument in some context, the photograph was taken on a Reflections session adjacent to our woodland one winter's day. The children are wearing warm, padded clothing and all are wearing gloves. The adults were aware of the car before the children found it and conducted a check to see what the hazards might be in case the children became interested. We made a decision that the car would be safe enough: that is, it was completely stable, there were no chemicals or sharp wires, but there was a little broken windscreen glass on the floor and one or two edges to consider. So, not completely without hazards, but with the probability that any risk to children would be minimal and something we could mitigate. In addition, we knew that the hazards would be worth discussing with the children.

Stellan giving advice about tornados

When the children showed an interest in the car, we asked them what they thought the dangers might be and gave them pointers about what to look out for. The children engaged in imaginative play in and around the ruined car, and we insisted they kept their gloves on. Perhaps the image of destruction prompted Stellan's reference to a tornado:

"We are running away from a twister. You have to run away." **Stellan**

After 10 minutes, at the children's request, we moved on further into the woodland. Following this session, we included the car photo in the diary which we emailed as usual to to the twelve parents whose children attended. The diary was sent at at 2.49pm; by 2.50pm we received a concerned email from a parent, raising her fears about the potential hazards. Her email had been copied to the other eleven parents who recieve the diary. We responded to them all with a full explanation and over the next 24 hours we received comments from a few of the other parents. Their views were overwhelmingly in support of our approach and showed considerable understanding of the choices we had made for their children:

"Dangers are everywhere and all we can hope is that with these experiences and freedom they learn to think, not assume."

"Let Forest School be a time for my child to explore whatever she can reach with a great team that is there to guide her."

"Having had two children go through the Forest School experience, I have to say that I have total and complete trust in Martin and the team and am aware of the benefit of allowing the children to explore their environment freely."

Parents of Forest School children

The mum who rasied the intial concerns subsequently responded to us saying that her child had explained the hazards to her and how to handle them. She also responded to the other parents saying her initial concerns may have been something of an over-reaction.

We are always grateful for parents who give us feedback, positive or negative. Their views help us to reflect more deeply on the choices we make for children in our care and this email was no exception. It became a pivotal moment for us as educators at Reflections. It helped us consider more deeply what we stand for in terms of our approach to hazards, risks and benefits. Following this incident and further reflection, we took a more robust stance to risk across the nursery:

"Forest School has enabled us to see the benefits of children taking their own risks…"

"…influenced our view of risk/benefit to the point where we are happy to provide risky activities in the indoors and outdoors which might otherwise not be provided."

Views of two Reflections' educators

Luke eating a snack in the oldest tree

Myeisha investigating a tree

The benefits of risky play

Risk is socially constructed, and what is acceptable in one situation or with one child might be unacceptable in another. When considering risk for children in your care, it is important to trust your own professional judgement on a case by case basis, taking into account what you know about a group of children, or an individual child. The better you know your children the better you will be at assessing appropriate risk for them:

> *"Providers should use their understanding of children's play needs, the need to offer risk and challenge and their own knowledge and experience to inform their judgements."*
>
> **Play England**

As with all choices we make for the children in our care, there are problems with creating environments for children which are risk-free. If we consider the image of the child as strong and competent then we are doing them a considerable disservice to take away any elements of risk from their play – something they may never recover from. Conversely, if we create a culture of low expectations of children then environments can become unstimulating and dull, potentially leading to adults managing children's behaviour. As Helen Tovey asserts:

> *"The danger of creating a supposedly risk-free environment is that the adults' expectations can remain low as children do not have the chance to demonstrate their confidence."*
>
> **Helen Tovey**

The links between risky play and areas of learning are supported by research. We know that children learn in different ways and that woodland experiences give children the opportunity to tune into what works for them. Pushing their own boundaries (and each other's), they can master complex skills. This also gives us as educators the opportunity to encourage 'growth mindsets'. Carol Dweck asserts that how you view yourself in relation to your own learning will affect how successful you are in life. If you believe that you learn from your mistakes, rather than having a fixed view of your abilities, then you are more likely to learn from them. And Tim Gill talks about 'learning accidents': non life-threatening accidents which all children need as part of their natural development. This applies to babies falling over when first trying to walk and onwards.

For educators at Reflections, providing elements of risky play is an extension of our values. We think that learning from risk and learning about risk is important. Children assessing and judging risk for themselves is just as critical to their learning as literacy and numeracy, if not more critical in terms of their physical development, which research shows is linked to psychological development.

Tim Gill refers to the "lost art of benign neglect" – an approach that does not involve the abdication of responsibility or a letting go of boundaries. On the contrary, it is about creating appropriate limits and boundaries whilst giving freedom within those limits for learning to occur. It is about watching, waiting and being considerate about the ways in which we intervene.

This naturally leads to the adult's responsibility when managing children's risk – when to intervene for their safety, and when not to intervene to support their learning. Over the years of operating a Forest School programme, our risk/benefits assessments have changed to reflect our approach, both in the woodland and in nursery.

Around the fire at Forest School

Sukie on the rope swing

Risky play in Reflections' nursery garden

Dynamic risk-benefit assessment

> *"Environments should be as safe as necessary, not as safe as possible."*
>
> **Royal Society of Prevention of Accidents (RoSPA).**

Tim Gill's framework for dynamic risk-benefit assessment involves minute-by-minute observations and potential interventions by adults who have responsibility for children. We have found it to be a useful approach to dealing with managing risk in a forest environment. Be aware, it puts the judgement and the responsibility directly in the hands of the educators who are in the field.

The critical factors that make it successful are training, experience and knowing the children in your care. Knowing each child and their abilities includes knowing their physical capabilities, their emotional resilience and their psychological approach. Of course, we can't know everything about each child, but it means making on-the-spot judgements about how to handle each situation based on what you do know. If a child is climbing a tree, how can you be sure that they will be safe? If the tree is wet and slippery will they still be safe?

How dangerous is it to slide down a hill in snow on your bottom? What if you decide to stand up and run down? The knowledge of each child in each situation is critical to supporting both their safety and their learning.

To support the adult's confidence and knowledge about children's abilities, it is critical that children generate a high awareness of risk assessment for themselves.

Mountain snow slide

Children assessing risk for themselves

In the forest, risks are assessed by adults and children together. Initially, most risk discussions with children will focus on nettles, brambles and fungi; what we do if we meet strangers or dogs in the woodland; and boundaries and water. When we are dealing with children's experiences we will discuss insects and other fauna when excavating; dead branches and trip hazards when exploring. We discuss safety around fires and ask children why it is important, and we show them how to light fires safely and put them out. We rarely introduce work with tools just for the sake of it — it tends to detract from their play. However, as adults we will use tools in the woodland, and children's curiosity frequently leads us to supporting them in, for example how to use a bow-saw. Children enjoy the sense of achievement of mastering such tools and work with them respectfully.

After many sessions in the woodland, most children acquire risk assessment skills as second nature and will readily point out hazards to their peers and to visiting adults:

Aidan climbing a tree

Putting out fires

Rohana and nettle leaves

Ben using a bowsaw

In the image below, Ashlei is crossing a homemade bridge for the first time. She is effectively assessing the risk for herself. So is Elliott, the child in the left of the picture, and you can see from his expression that he is probably deciding against it for now.

It is worth noting that very few children are reckless, and if you are aware of the one or two children who may have a tendency to treat risk in a cavalier fashion then you will be able to deal with them effectively, too.

> "One's light and one's dark." Rohana, telling the difference between stinging nettles and other plant leaves nearby
>
> "Stinging nettles! Over there… Holly leaves, they look spiky! Sticks – they bonk!!" Kyra
>
> "You can't touch the edge, it's spiky. You can touch the soft part." Arden
>
> "Dead sticks falling on our heads!" Lachlan

Children work in the realm of the real and the imagined, and will often add risks of their own:

> "We need to watch out for hedgehogs as they have prickly backs!" Ella
>
> "You have to be careful of the tigers!…I'm not scared of the tigers." Thomas

Regular discussions about risk with children in the woodland are often extended to their physical experiences. Most children quickly become very physically adept in the woodland. In the early weeks, as they acclimatise to the environment, they will frequently trip and will approach climbing trees quite tentatively. After about five weeks they will have made the woodland their own and many will independently explore the forest, build dens, play on a rope swing, climb and jump off trees, scale steep hills and slide or roll down, play hide and seek and cross homemade bridges.

Bridge crossing

Elliot watching Ashlei cross the bridge

Transforming effects of Forest School

> The outdoors offers a perfect companion to provision indoors, working in harmony and providing a complementary environment that enhances and extends what we are able to give children inside.
>
> **Jan White**[xxxv]

As educators, we were aware that Forest School offered us an opportunity to develop our pedagogy; however, we were unaware of all the lessons it could teach us. We wanted to ensure that woodland experiences were not simply a bolt-on addition to our approach, separate to our work indoors or in the garden, but we were not always clear about how to integrate our learning from the forest into the nursery.

The first time we encountered ripple effects from Forest School experiences was when we received a photo from parents of two children who attended our very early pilot programme. They had taken the children to Scotland on holiday and had enjoyed a relaxed day at the beach whilst their children spent hours building numerous 'fairy dens' with the available resources. They (and we) were delighted that Forest School had clearly influenced their children's learning.

Fairy den on the beach

Ruby and the fire square (Reflections 2009)

We also noticed that Forest School became a significant topic of discussion amongst friends at nursery with children explaining to friends what goes on in the forest. We had discussed with the children the dangers of leaving fires unattended in the woodland, and one afternoon Ruby was playing in the Construction Room in nursery. She was working with Jenga bricks and Lego people and talking with her friends about camp fires in the woodland:

> *"I'm making the fire square like we have at Forest School. I made the fire like Martin does."*

Making a fire square

Seated around the fire

Ruby selected some tissue paper in red, yellow and orange. She ripped the paper into small pieces and placed them in the centre of her square, on top of the waffle of Jenga bricks. "This is the fire."

Ruby showed her friends what she was doing:

> *"I made the fire like Martin and we have a fire square. Be careful, the fire is hot. "*

She explained to one of the educators, Shelley (who also attends Forest School) what she had been doing:

> *"These are the children sitting eating lunch around the fire. This is Martin, he looks after the fire. This is you Shelley. You, erm, look after us and feed us."*

After 30 minutes, Ruby pushed aside her creation and bits went everywhere, including a splash of red, yellow and orange tissue paper. Shelley asked her if she had finished playing.

> *"No. This is what happens if you leave the fire in the forest!"*

We recognised that the relationship between forest experiences and nursery is important to the children, and we sought further opportunities to deepen this connection.

Consequences of an unattended fire

Forest School influences: transforming environments

Nursery garden

Our first step was to seek to understand the children's view of the forest more deeply. We gave the children cameras to record the things they liked in the forest.

Amelie and Katie sharing photos

The majority of the children took photos of the adults, each other, leaves, open spaces, and flora and fauna. Even the minibus and the Forest School sandwiches were popular. Many of the children had taken photos of the climbing trees, and the fireplace also featured frequently.

Photograph of the climbing tree by Lucas (3:11)

Tree photograph by Amelie (3:10)

In addition, we reviewed the discussions we have at the end of each session when we ask what children have enjoyed, and the climbing tree and fires were again particularly popular.

Following these investigations, we took some time to reconsider our garden environment to see if we could bring these aspects of the woodland to nursery, much as they have done in the Danish Schools we visited (see Chapter 2). In 2012, a tree needed felling in the nursery garden. Fallen trees form the principal climbing areas for the children in the woodland and we are aware of how beneficial these are, providing knobbly, uneven surfaces for children to really test their skills:

> *"When the distance between all the rungs in a climbing net or a ladder is exactly the same, the child has no need to concentrate on where he puts his feet. Standardisation is dangerous because play becomes simplified and the child does not have to worry about his movements. This lesson cannot be carried over to all the knobbly and asymmetrical forms, with which one is confronted throughout life."*
>
> **Helle Nebolong, Danish designer of natural playgrounds**

We retained as much of the tree trunk as we could realistically move, and children immediately showed interest. They initially constructed ladders as we often do in the woodland, with some adult assistance, in order to scale the tree.

Yasmina on the ladder

Bridge in Reflections' garden

With branches culled from our local woodland, we later constructed what became known as the 'bridge' in the nursery garden.

The bridge has become one of the most significant resources for children aged 2 to 5 in nursery and is recognised as such by the educators:

> "They have surprised me how well they can cope with the need to balance and negotiate their way across the bridge.... I underestimated the benefits to my age group when it was first created, so it has been a great surprise!"
>
> **Reflections' educator**

Taking into account the children's fascination with fires in the woodland, and inspired by the Danish approach to having a fire burning in the garden on most days, we installed a fire pit in the nursery garden that is now used every day in winter.

We provide warm apple soup (apple juice with gnocchi) or mulled juice for the nursery children outdoors on cold days, and we often notice the gentle aroma of wood smoke during our outdoor experiences.

Trying out the bridge

Warm apple soup in the nursery garden

We were inspired by a design for a sand and water area, which we saw both at Høndruphus and Laerkereden both in Denmark (see Chapter 2 and below).

Made from halved logs, ours resembles a Heath Robinson aqueduct, which the children love to dam with sand and watch it overflow. Apart from its woodland look, the irregular surfaces make for more complex play.

Reflections' sand and water area

Laerkereden water area

Children in the woodland will often spend significant time experimenting with ways to cross a ditch. One child, whose parents were coming to the woodland to see the last Forest School session in the programme, was so determined to master the complex skill of balancing on two branches before they arrived, that she repeatedly fell off. She finally suceeded and proudly demonstrated her new-found skill to her parents. Knowing the benefits a ditch can bring, we dug out a modest-sized hole in the nursery garden which the children now experiment with daily.

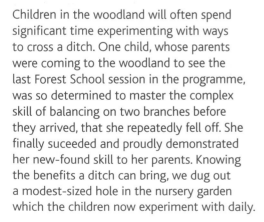

Ditch in Reflections' garden

Jan White visited Reflections and we discussed some of the elements that children were engaging with in the context of our woodland work, one of which was 'prospect' – the delight in being enclosed and seeing out. We created the (now ubiquitous) willow den with this in mind, and made it part of a nature trail which the children follow amongst other bushes in the garden.

The same idea of prospect informed our design for a tepee made from woodland timber, which we often cover with leaves or material – it provides a shaded area in the summer.

Teepee and bridge in Reflections' garden

Hiding in the willow den

Reflections' side garden

Interest table

Outdoor stove

Outdoor room

In 2013 we created an outdoor room in our side garden for the 2 to 3 year olds' group. Here children write, draw, read, eat, sculpt, climb, grow their own vegetables, or simply play in the mud, all year round. As winter approached we installed a log-burning stove and the children created their own safety rules, including who could set it alight and keep it stoked up.

Toddler bridge

Claywork in the outdoor room

Edible garden

"Everything in nature flows in cycles and spirals."
Chris Holland

In late 2009, one of the children in pre-school asked: "Where do chips come from?" – and another child replied, "From McDonalds". This discussion went on to prompt a project about potatoes. The conversation also immediately signified that we had some work to do in order to deepen their understanding of food, growing and nature. We noted that in the forest, children often discussed the cycles of nature, seeking to understand the seasons and what happens next at any time of year.

Following the potato project, we decided to create part of the garden into an edible landscape where children could learn about planting, growing, harvesting and the rhythm of the seasons.

Lachlan picking beans

Edible garden

Making clay wishes

By autumn 2010 the children did some late planting in tubs, giving them a harvest of potatoes in time for Christmas lunch. We planted fruit trees with the children in the front garden and they made clay 'wishes' to plant with each tree and buried them under the roots.

Inspired by the book *The Edible Schoolyard* and a visit to Child First Nursery in Northampton, which has a rich and well developed growing area, we acquired a large greenhouse. In winter 2010 we added composting bins and raised beds and we planted espaliered fruits along our flint wall. During 2011 and 2012 the children enjoyed planting seeds and pricking them out, and then re-planting them in the raised beds.

Watering seedlings

Trying nastertiums

Observing peas

Planting the tree wishes

Following each harvest, the children have enjoyed the fruits of their labour, such as making soups from the vegetables they grow. In 2013, in discussion with the children, we selected more exotic fruit and vegetables including physalis and cucamelons, a cross between a cucumber and a melon – the children loved them!

Picking tomatoes

Forest School influences: transforming practice

Our garden has always included many open-ended resources, especially crates, logs, branches and bricks, which we know enrich the children's experiences and provide useful tools when working on projects.

> "In any environment, both the degree of inventiveness and creativity, and the possibility of discovery, are directly proportional to the number and kind of variables in it."
> Simon Nicholson

The range of resources both indoors and outdoors influenced a project that began in July 2012 and which illustrates the dialogue between forest and nursery, and shows how environments can contribute to a holistic approach to learning. In Denmark, this is an important part of their pedagogy and they give high regard to the "physical, psychological and aesthetic elements of the indoor and outdoor environments". (Williams-Siegfredsen).

The following is an exerpt from a larger project involving over 50 children over a 12–month period.

Teddy making cement

Teddy, Leila and the water feature: a conversation between forest and nursery (Reflections 2012/13)

Teddy and Leila often worked with each other, and shortly before the project began they were building together in the garden using polystyrene blocks. It was windy and they were having some problems:

> "My wall, it keep falling over. The wind do it, they fall on the floor." Teddy (3:0)
>
> "My need cement, cement like a builder." Teddy

Teddy used his spade to stir sand, clay and water together before filling his bucket up with it again.

> "My did it, my a builder!" Teddy
>
> "I am making a castle, look how tall it can go." Leila (2:7)

An educator asked Leila what she thought would happen if the wind blew.

> "It wouldn't fall down, Teddy makes strong sticky clay so it won't blow away, and I am making some strong sticky clay like Teddy's for my castle!" Leila

Leila building with clay

Exploring ideas for a water feature

In July 2012, a group of children were constructing in the garden with natural resources. Leo had an idea to construct a helicopter. The children decided to build it under the teepee. Some children selected stones and Teddy placed pieces of wood around the stones and commented:

"Look! I made a water feature!" Teddy (3:1)

An older boy, Ewan, was sceptical about it working and shared his theory of its failure.

"It won't work; the water will just soak into the mud." Ewan (4:8)

"We need to block it with wood." Teddy

The children discovered that the wood didn't contain the water. After many attempts, Ewan insisted:

"This doesn't really work, we need to plan first." Ewan

To support their planning, we introduced the children to an Andy Goldsworthy book with images of water and they created designs for containing water.

"I wanted it to look like this one…" Teddy

In July and August 2012, Teddy was experimenting in the nursery garden with water retention:

Working both indoors and out, the children created a water feature using plasticine.

"We need to make a row of bridges for the water to go under." Teddy

Teddy's idea of bridges was one which persisted throughout his work on the water feature.

Experimenting with water retention   *Teddy and the plasticine bridges*

In September 2012, the Forest School programme recommenced and Teddy and Leila were in the same group attending weekly woodland sessions.

Teddy and Leila investigating water

In the forest, the children immediately encountered water:

> *"Look a big puddle."* **Teddy**
>
> *"Wow, look a bridge! We need one of these in our water feature."* **Teddy**

By early October 2012, Teddy was working in the forest with his friends, refining ideas for the water feature.

> *"It's a tie bridge. Do you like it guys?"* **Teddy**
>
> *"Our idea worked! It can go in our water feature."* **Teddy**

"It worked!"

Teddy's 'tie bridge'

In November, Teddy and Leila worked with friends on a prototype watercourse in the garden.

Testing a brick watercourse

By January, Leila was designing fairy houses in the woodland:

Leila's fairy house

'Fairies' was a persistent theme which Leila sought to include in the water feature.

> *"Look at my fairy house. The fairies can go into it. The big sticks are for the garden. The little sticks are the houses."*
> **Leila (3:2)**

Back in the nursery, Teddy was refining the brick design, using Jenga blocks.

Teddy working with Jenga bricks

Indoors, the children were given foil trays, pebbles and other resources to design their own water features. Teddy and Leila were working at the same table and negotiating design ideas - Teddy still keen on bridges and Leila still keen on fairies.

Planning water features

Leila worked on her design ideas: "I want three circles, one big, one small and one medium-sized." Leila

Leila drawing a water feature

By March 2013, Leila and Teddy were working on watercourses together in the garden:

Teddy and Leila working on a water course

Testing water courses

In May 2013, something exciting happened in the woodland. Teddy and Leila alighted upon a series of bracket fungi and Teddy had a Eureka! moment:

"Big mushrooms!" Teddy

"They look like giant footsteps." Leila

"Water feature! The water could go down the mushrooms!!" Teddy

Bracket fungus in the forest

Bracket fungus inspired design

Leila drawing on acetate

Reviewing bracket fungus photos

The children poured water down the fungi and followed the path it took.

We brought photographs of the fungi back to nursery and the children began to work on a fungi-inspired design for the water feature.

Leila continued design work on acetate and projected her plans across the room for her friends, using the overhead projector.

In May 2013, the children were planning the location in the garden and laying out their jointly-agreed designs.

Negotiation continued:

"I would like the circles in a line." Leila

"No that's boring, we need them to be in zig-zags." Teddy

Leila thought for a little while: "You're right Teddy. We should have it zig-zagged." Leila

The children met with a landscape gardener, Andy, who was to build the water feature to their design. There were many animated conversations – Teddy never got his bridge and Leila never added her fairies – but the final design was agreed by consensus.

The children oversaw the construction adding comments and instruction:

"Only green plants... I suppose it's OK." Teddy

Leila's design, projected

Bin lid water feature

Teddy with a brick layout

Teddy and Leila meeting Andy

Overseeing the build process

Leila and Teddy cutting the tape

A year after its inception, the forest-fungi-inspired water feature was completed and opened by Teddy and Leila with children, staff and parents and friends on the 26th July 2013: a gift to the nursery garden from the children, with inspiration from the forest.

Official opening of the water feature

Sculpture focus: ice (Reflections 2013/14)

During winter 2013/14 we had a focus on sculpture across the whole nursery, and for the older children this work spanned both forest and nursery. Children will encounter ice in the woodland but less so in the nursery garden, so we decided to bring an ice sculptor to the setting.

Children will have the chance to create many sculptures in nursery by modelling (the addition of materials such as clay or Plasticine), but will not have as many opportunities for sculpture by carving (reduction by the removal of material). During the sculpture focus we had given them soap, fruit and vegetables, wax, chalk blocks, wood and small pieces of ice to work on, and we saw an ice sculpture demonstration as a useful way of supporting their investigations and provoking further carving work, as well as continuing the dialogue between forest and nursery.

As our sculpture melted it became a giant lolly for the children to engage with. Since then, at nursery, we have been working with Sara Stanley, author of *Why Think?*, to deepen or questions to children. One of the questions we have been asking them is: Now that the ice has melted, where has the sculpture gone?

Tanya carving ice

James touching the sculpture

Sophie-Grace exploring the ice

Queenie and Leila using different senses to investigate the ice

Studying the ice

John, sculpting

Engaging with the finished sculpture

Selected bibliography and further reading

Ackerman, D. (1999) *Deep Play*. Random House, New York

Bruce, T. (1991) *Time to Play in Early Childhood Education*. Hodder and Stoughton, London

Constable, C. (2012) *The Outdoor Classroom Ages 3-7*. Routledge, Abingdon

Chick, A. (2011) *Crocodiles*. On Reflection Publishing, Worthing

Chick, A. (2011) *Light Everywhere!* On Reflection Publishing, Worthing

Clouder, C and Rawson, M. (1998) *Waldorf Education*. Floris, Edinburgh

Csikszentmihalyi, M. (1990) *Flow: the psychology of optimal experience*. Harper Collins, New York

Doyle, J. & Milchem, K. (2012) *Developing a Forest School in Early Years Provision*. Practical Pre-School Books, London

Gill, T. (2007) *No Fear: Growing Up in a Risk Averse Society*. CGF, London

Holland, C. (2009) *I love my World*. Wholeland Press, Otterton

Knight, S. (2009) (2013) *Forest Schools and Outdoor Learning in the Early Years*. Sage, London

Knight, S. (2011) *Risk and Adventure in Early Years Outdoor Play*. Sage, London

Kutch, I & Walden, B. (2001) *Winter: nature activities for children*. Floris, Edinburgh

Kutch, I & Walden, B. (2005) *Spring: nature activities for children*. Floris, Edinburgh

Louv, R. (2005) *Last Child in the Woods*. Atlantic Books, London

Malaguzzi, L. (1993) *History, ideas and basic philosophy:* an interview with Lella Gandini. In: C. Edwards, L. Gandini and G. Forman (Eds) The Hundred Languages of Children. Ablex, Norwood

Dweck, C. (2000). *Self-theories: their role in motivation, personality and development*. Psychology Press, Hove

Murray, R. and O'Brien, W. (2006) 'Such enthusiasm – A joy to see'. *An Evaluation of Forest Schools in England*. Report to the Forestry Commission by New Economic Foundation and Forest Research. Farnham

Nebolong, H. (2004) *Nature's Playground*. Green Places

Nicholson, S. (1971) '*How NOT to cheat children: the theory of loose parts.*' Landscape Architecture, October 30-34

Ouvry, M. (2003) *Exercising muscles and minds*. National Children's Bureau, London

Rinaldi, C. (2008) *In Dialogue with Reggio Emilia*. Routledge, Abingdon

Robson, S. (2006) *Developing Thinking and Understanding in Young Children*. Routledge, Abingdon

Stanley, S. (2012) *Why Think?* Continuum, London

Thornton, L. & Brunton, P. (2005) (2009) *Understanding the Reggio Approach*. David Fulton, Abingdon

Thornton, L. & Brunton, P. (2011) *Making the most of Outdoor Learning*. Bloomsbury, London

Tovey, H. (2007) *Playing Outdoors: Spaces and Places, Risk and Challenge*. Open University Press, Maidenhead

Waters, A. (1999) *The Edible Schoolyard: Learning in the real world*. Abe Books, Canada

White, J. (2008) *Playing and Learning Outdoors*. Routledge, Abingdon

Williams-Siegfredsen, J. (2012) *Understanding the Danish Forest School Approach*. Routledge, Abingdon

Photographic acknowledgements

Thanks to Cath Reding from Sightlines Initiative for selected images from Høndruphus, Laerkereden, Lille Dalby and Globussen schools, Denmark.

Image of Chelsea Open Air Nursery courtesy of themselves.

Image of beach fairy dens by a parent at Reflections.

Photography by educators, children and parents at Reflections Nursery and especially Lyndsey Ridgwell, Teresa Grimaldi, Shelley Barton, Harrie Jones, Angela Chick, Laura Magnavacchi, Kathryn Jordan and Caroline Watts. All other photography by the author.

Schematic of *How we tend to work at Reflections* by author; drawn by Angela Chick.

Notes

[i] McMillan, M., cited in Ouvry, M. (2008:14)

[ii] Ouvry, M. (2003)

[iii] http://www.naturalengland.org.uk/Images/Childhood%20 and%20Nature%20Survey_tcm6-10515.pdf

[iv] Louv, R. (2005)

[v] White, J. (2008)

[vi] Tovey, H. (2007)

[vii] 'Forest School' is a UK description. Danish Schools with a strong outdoor focus are called Skovbørnehave (forest kindergarten); Skovgruppe (forest group) or Naturbørnehave (nature kindergarten)

[viii] http://www.ecoventureme.com/fs/fieldstudies.html

[ix] The Forest Education Initiative (FEI) in Scotland and Wales and now the Forest Education Network (FEN) in England are all part of the Great Britain FEI. See: http://www.foresteducation. org/

[x] Knight, S. (2009)

[xi] Cited in: Williams-Siegfredsen, J. (2012:8)

[xii] http://www.chelseaopenairnursery.co.uk/

[xiii] Constable, K. (2012)

[xiv] Murray, R. and O'Brien, I. (2005)

[xv] Grahn, P., cited in: 'Outdoor Learning', Education Scotland. http://www.educationscotland.gov.uk/Images/ OutdoorLearningSupport1_tcm4-740873.pdf

[xvi] White, J. (2008)

[xvii] http://www.foresteducation.org/woodland_learning/

[xviii] Secret Garden Outdoor Nursery Visitor Protocol: http://www.secretgardenoutdoor-nursery.co.uk/Visitor%20 Protocol.pdf

[xix] 'The forest school; a thrilling and inspiring environment for preschool children': Fleetwood's Charity Pre-School Group URN: 583731 Ofsted Good Practice Example: Early Years http://www.plymouth.gov.uk/documents-gpforestschool.pdf

[xx] http://www.edsup.co.uk/ArticleView.aspx?pid=344

[xxi] Malaguzzi, L. (1993)

[xxii] http://www.aldofortunati.it/

[xxiv] A reference to the poem, "No Way The Hundred is there", by Loris Malaguzzi

[xxv] Rinaldi, cited in Thornton and Brunton (2005:16)

[xxvii] Bruce, T. (1991)

[xxviii] Robson, S. (2006)

[xxix] Play Safety Forum, 'Managing risk in play provision: A position statement' http://www.playengland.org.uk/ media/120462/managing-risk-play-safety-forum.pdf

[xxx] http://www.freeplaynetwork.org.uk/pubs/risk.pdf p.78

[xxxi] Tovey, H. (2007:101)

[xxxii] Dweck, C. (2000).

[xxxiii] Gill, T. (2007)

[xxxiv] http://www.rospa.com/schoolandcollegesafety/info/ managing-safety-schools-colleges.pdf

[xxxv] White, J. (2008:2)

[xxxvi] Nebelong, H. (2004:30)

[xxxvii] Holland, C. (2009:12)

[xxxviii] Waters, A. (1999)

[xxxix] Nicholson, S. (1971)

[xl] Williams Siegfredsen, J. (2012)